It's Over For Here!

It is time to take your head out of the sand and move forward!

Deborah A. Wright

It's Over for Here!

Copyright © 2008 by Deborah A. Wright

First Edition August 2010
Second Edition July, 2015

Printed in the United States of America

ISBN 978-0-615-24549-2
Published by: Parablist Ministries Inc.
Parablist Publishing House, Inc.
Richmond Heights, OH 44143
www.parablistbooksonline.com
Email: parablistpublishing@yahoo.com

Unless otherwise indicated, Bible quotations are taken from the King James Version of the Bible.

Dedication

I dedicate this book to my Lord and Savior Jesus Christ, the lover of my soul. It is my heart's desire to press towards the mark of the high calling you have placed on my life and to be a reflection of all that YOU are, in the eyes of those I encounter along the way. Thank you Lord.

Acknowledgments

I thank God I have finally completed my first book. I also wish to thank some very important people who lived through the writing of the chapters with me, my mom, Ruth Hester, who never failed to believe in me and encourage me; my four bright and beautiful children, Jarisia, Gayla, Yolanda and James, my son-in-laws, Maurice and Thomas and also my step-son and daughter-in law, Lonnie Jr. and Erika, I am proud of you all; and to my twelve grandchildren and two great grandchildren, Michayla and DeAaron, Jr. you guys make good story material, (smile). A special shout-out goes to my "Mr. Wright", Lonnie and much love to my dear friends Carol Greer, Char Kelso and Linda Sims for rescuing me several times over the years.

I further acknowledge my beloved father, the late Elder Harvey L. Hester Sr. and my precious grandmother, Mary E. Creagh.   You both taught me so much. I now understand what Dad was trying to teach me about, "holding the spoon".   To my Sistahs in ministry, Janice Renee Erving, Lynn Mays, Pamelia Tyree-Carr and Dr. Jori Maccarthy who kept the fire under my feet to finish this project…thanks.

Special thanks to my brothers, remarkable Men of God, Harvey, Sylvester, Kevin and Darrell whose love, patience, life lessons and "sister support" energize me. Last but certainly not least, my baby sister Letitia. I am so proud of the strong, beautiful woman you have become. Much love to you all!

It's Over for Here!
Contents

Section I
Take Your Head Out Of The Sand...

Section II
...And Move Forward!

Introduction

This book is a guide for "grown folk" who have messed up repeatedly in areas of finance, relationship choices, career paths and spiritually. Although you may have messed up multiple times in one or more areas of your life, it is not too late to get it together. Once you begin to see yourself as God sees you and embrace who He has uniquely created you to be, doors of opportunity will swing open for you.

You ARE important and this is the right book for you. Not only will you learn to celebrate who God has created you to be. You will learn to embrace the purpose He has called you to fulfill.

Are you tired of being able to see what you want in life, but never quite able to map out a plan to get there? Well, this book is your first step to a lifestyle "re-mix". The first chapters are in the section entitled, "Take Your Head Out of the Sand...". The other chapters are in the section entitled, "...And Move Forward".

I am sure someone might ask, "What do those section titles mean?" Well, let us look at two examples in nature. The ostrich buries his head in the sand leaving his hind parts out in the open. The flamingo spends long stretches of time standing on one leg. A lot of people have unknowingly adopted both of these stances.

Like the ostrich, they have become oblivious to what is going on around them. Even worse yet, they bury their heads in fear and denial, while their hind parts are out in the open for all to see.

It's Over for Here!

Like the flamingo, they have become accustomed to instability in their lives and have even adapted instability as their permanent stance. It is not possible to move forward successfully on one leg. Some researchers believe the flamingo stands on one leg to conserve energy. They find themselves guilty of this as well. They may not be happy "**here**", but if it means breaking a sweat to move forward, it is not going to happen.

Some people feel that they have to dig their heels in deep to withstand the storms that come their way. On one leg, it is so easy for even the smallest wave to wipe them out. By adopting this stance, going through life with only one leg to stand on, even the greatest plans and dreams are doomed for eventual failure!

For many people, when it comes to finances, they feel if they ignore it, just maybe it will go away. Stacks of bills go unopened. They depend on devices such as privacy manager and caller I.D. to aid them in hiding out. Many people have abandoned having landlines in their home as an effort to avoid "Bill". Cell phones serve the purpose for most. They can keep their lines of communication open and control access to the number. The truth is, although they may think they are hiding, their tail feathers are flapping in the wind.

Now, most people really would like to get out of this rut, once and for all. They do not like this stance. What is it that keeps them always a day late and a dollar short? Some people find themselves in bankruptcy court again, divorce court again, another foreclosure, another eviction, shut off notices every other month, NSF accounts, where does it end?

The desire to change is there, but success seems just a fleeting illusion, always just beyond our reach. Some may even feel doomed for failure and blame one of the mentalities named in Chapter Two, the "Struggling Mentality", the "Po Folks Mentality", the "Lottery Mentality" or the "Grandma 'nem Mentality". If this introduction is describing you, help is on the way.

Section One.
Take your Head Out of the Sand...

This section gently nudges you into taking a stark look at your present situation. The Chapters in Section One should give you the courage to take your head out of the sand once and for all. We cannot experience God's best for us fearful or in denial of the circumstances around us. You are sick and tired of being sick and tired. You know in your heart that God must have had more in store for your life than what you have experienced so far. Well, if you feel a slight tapping on your shoulder, this book is for you. What you need to do is shake the sand out of your hair and keep reading.

Section Two.
...And Move Forward!

Until you put your foot down on behaviors that keep you spiraling in frustration, you will not be able to stop this cycle. Many people find themselves in the same position as the flamingo. They become accustomed to instability. However, they cannot survive the trials and storms that await them standing on one foot. The next gust of wind will blow them right down. This section helps you set

It's Over for Here!

forth a plan to get on a solid path to stability in finances, relationships, health, career and most importantly your spiritual life. This section guides you through setting out a plan of action to get on stable footing, finally.

You made the first step in the right direction. You have begun a journey towards your personal path of success for the rest of your life.

You might have responded that all of this sounds good, but what is going to break the cycle of broken resolutions that has plagued most of us, all of our adult lives?

First, and foremost, we must REPENT. The act of repenting lets God know we are serious this time. Secondly, we must SUBMIT. Submit our will and our way to the Father's will.

Jesus spoke some powerful words on the cross, "Let thy will be done". Look at what transpired after those words were spoken. Instantly the doors to our salvation, deliverance and healing were opened. When we say, "Let thy will be done", we are surrendering to God's will and immediately the red carpet is rolled out and we walk directly into the realm of God's possibilities for our lives!

Though we may stumble and fall a few times, God's grace and mercy will see us through as long as we are sincere about making a change and stay surrendered to His will. In the Bible, Jesus told the woman to go and sin no more. The scriptures also say, "Whom the Son sets free, is free indeed". True deliverance is possible to those who simply believe and turn from all of their old habits. So, all of you who are truly serious this time, throw your hands up and waive the white flag, deliverance is on the way!

It's Over for Here!

When you truly surrender, watch God move! Your life will begin to shift and line up with His plan for your life. You are God's gift to the world and He desires you to be the best you can be. Come on now, let's get started because truly it is over for **"here"**!

"Here" represents any place or situation in your life that is stagnant, destructive or barren."

It's Over for Here!

Section I
Take Your Head Out of the Sand

Chapter One

Out of the Mouth of Babes

1

Out of the Mouth of Babes

My granddaughter was my inspiration for the title of this book. When she was about 3 years old, she was visiting her other grandmother for the weekend. During the course of her visit, she had crossed the line with her grandmother one too many times and was chastised.

Her grandmother's actions took her by surprise. She was outdone. After bouncing upstairs gathering her overnight case, she marched to the front door. Seeing that it was now night and not time for anyone to pick her up, her grandmother was confused and asked her, "NyKeara, where are you going?" With all of the sincerity and boldness of a 3 year old, she looked her grandma straight in the face and answered, "I don't know, but it's over for here!"

What an answer for a small child! How many times as adults have we continued to stay in situations as opposed to moving on? We were too afraid to move on out of fear. The three year old had no fear of the dark outside. The fact that she did not know her way home or have cab fare did not sway her decision. All she knew was that, in her opinion, "here" was not a good place for her right now.

It's Over for Here!

For this book, "here" represents any place or situation in your life that is stagnant, destructive or barren. Being "here" keeps you from moving forward in the things God has called you to do or be.

Many people have stayed in abusive relationships until it was too late, simply because for them, the "known" (present level of violence) was better than the unknown, (lack of financial security). Some people never even attempted certain jobs or promotions because the bird in the hand was easier than the one in the bush. How many people have settled for a broke-legged pigeon not realizing a prize catch was just a few thorns away?

I have often wondered about the story of Cinderella. If her evil stepmother and stepsisters were so good at making her life miserable, why did she care about the fancy dress turning back into rags or the horses back into mice? She should have realized that she was already in the palace!

Imagine what could have happened if Cinderella had called the Prince to the side at about a quarter till and said, "Hey Prince, let's talk." She could have told him her story and if he was interested, at 12:01, she would have still been in the palace. He could have at the snap of his finger ordered out another dress. On the other hand, if at 5 minutes before, he did not seem interested she could have caught the first carriage going her way.

One thing for sure is that all of you reading this book are older than 3 years old, quite a bit older. Do not feel bad if you are a little late getting it. One good thing is that it does not matter when you finally "get it" just as long as you get it. Once you get it, you can move forward with the rest of your life.

So, are you still not sure whether this book is for you? Is it that you do not want to admit it? Well after you read this section, you will know for sure.

21 REASONS YOU KNOW THINGS ARE MESSED UP:

1.

Shut off notices are a frequent occurrence at your household. You know what "checking for trouble means".

2.

You have had 3 different phone numbers in the past 5 years and live in the same house.

3.

You belong to the "Twenty Dolla Holla Club". You and eight friends call to borrow $20.00 back and forth before payday. (That is if either of you has $20.00 before payday.)

4.

You have utilities in someone else's name. (How is it that the light bill is in Little Jimmy's name? He is only two years old.)

5.

On most days, you struggle to find $3.00 toll money in your $400.00 designer purse.

6.

You have put $5.00 worth of gas in your luxury vehicle.

7.

You had to rummage through the pockets of five suits and a winter coat to scrounge up $5.42. You were too ashamed to put the .42 in the tank so you stopped at $5.00.

8.

You regularly go out and have a nice meal, but sneak out past the waitress because you cannot afford to leave a decent tip.

9.

You have several items on your credit report that total less than this year's Easter outfit.

10.

You have robbed, choked and molested your piggy bank on more than one occasion for a diet soda.

11.

You have been on every "safe" diet on the market and have five different sizes of clothes in your closet.

12.

You have a prized collection of exercise equipment with every gadget known to Midnight Shopper's Network enshrined in your spare bedroom.

13.

You believe that shaving 15 or 20 pounds from your true weight for the driver's license bureau is faith. You were just calling those things that are not as though they were.

14.

You have been engaged to the man of your dreams for fourteen years, (minus the times you broke up, like your birthday, most major holidays and when his four children were born).

15.

The people on this job are terrible just like the ones on the other five jobs.

16.

You believe that a "disability check" is God's modern day manna. Manna was the menu for the wilderness. Milk and honey was on the menu for the Promised Land. It is strange that your healing came after the disability determination.

17.

You dodge communion at least once or twice a year. You mysteriously have to work or you shoot your finger in the air and tip out early. You were just weak that night. You did not plan to sin.

18.

Your life is like a country western song. Everything that has not died yet ran away with a stranger in a pickup truck.

19.

You finally realized that getting in the "Unspoken Request" prayer line is more private that the "All who have sinned and come short of the Glory of God" prayer line. (There is no sense in flaunting your sin before the whole congregation! Remember in the Old Testament how a sinner had to drag his sin sacrifice through the middle of town to the temple—everybody knew he had messed up!

20.

You complain about your job 5 of the 8 hours you are there, but have not attempted to make a change in nearly 10 years.

It's Over for Here!

21.

You hid this book under a package of plus sized underwear in your cart so that no one would see you purchasing it.

Ouch! I am sure a lot of you found yourself somewhere in this section. There is no need to be embarrassed. Like the ostrich, those around you already know. As for those of you still too shy to pull your head out of the sand just cover the book neatly with a brown paper bag and keep reading.

It's Over for Here!

Chapter Two

Changing Mentalities

2

Changing Mentalities

The Struggling Mentality

People with a Struggling Mentality feel that their whole life's purpose is to struggle along barely making it, year after year. They never have enough to make ends meet. If they have bacon, they just ran out of eggs. When they have coffee, they just ran out of cream.

In actuality, they have become so accustomed to struggling that they have developed a lifestyle around it. They have gotten used to utility shut-offs, running out of basic necessities and not being able to participate in the simple pleasures of life.

They have unconsciously sabotaged themselves by living for today and failing to plan. They refuse to stick to a budget. They give in to their taste buds and eat filet mignon when their budget calls for meat loaf surprise. By the end of the week, they are down to sardines and ramen noodles.

Everything in their lives is feast or famine. When they do occasionally come across some extra money, they splurge, rationalizing that this chance may not come again. "Live for today", is their motto. They believe that the only thing promised for tomorrow is more struggling.

The Po' Folk's Mentality

These people do not even have the energy or desire to struggle. They feel, why bother. They do not look for life to get any better. Everybody on this side of the tracks is poor. They have marked out their territory in the "Land of Po", and this is their lot in life. To them, it is like a caste system. Once you are born into this class, you die in this class.

For people with the "Po Folk's Mentality" struggling is unnecessary. Their thinking is similar to a bug trapped in a jar. They feel that if you got a few holes in the top so you can breath be thankful. You can view the world outside from within the glass, but you ain't getting out! Junebug tried it and it didn't work for him. So why should you butt your head trying to get out? It may be limited in here, but at least it is safe from everything that lies out there.

It never even dawns on people with a "Po' Folk's Mentality" that it is possible that they could be released. Any number of things could happen. It is possible the lid could suddenly open allowing their escape or the jar could suddenly fall and break allowing their exit. But, instead of them believing anything good could happen, they have bought into the perceived notion that when it comes to the good life, a better life, all they can do is look out past the glass.

A funny thing about some people with a "Po' Folk's Mentality", is that they do not even complain. As long as they got grits, gravy and a hog or two, everything is just fine. (Somebody has got to be at the bottom, right?)

The Gender Mentality

People with this mentality blame being born male or female as the source of their problems. A man might say, "Women get all of the breaks!" Whereas, a woman would make the excuse, "I bet I could break that glass ceiling if I were a man". They live their entire lives bitter, angry and blaming the other gender for their personal shortcomings. The problem with people in this group is that they refuse to take responsibility for who they are. Instead of putting forth the extra effort it may take, it is easier to blame someone else.

God in His infinite wisdom created each person exactly the way He wanted them to be. He also equipped each person with the skills and temperaments required to pursue their intended purpose. He determined your gender. You are fearfully and wonderfully made in His image. Enjoy the life God has planned for you. Dig your roots in deep and push out those blooms for the world to see.

The Grandma 'Nem Mentality

This crew truly believes that the apple does not fall far from the tree. They base their entire lives on what Grandma 'nem did. If their ancestors were always struggling, they feel that this is also their lot in life. If Grandpa was a bum, then Little Billie will be too. If nobody in their family finished school, why should they be the one to break the mold? They are satisfied with Momma's ole time religion and everything else. It's just fine with them.

It's Over for Here!

People with this mentality do not even realize times change. Each generation should strive to do better. The Bible says that fathers should leave an inheritance to their children. So, take that bumper sticker declaring you are spending your children's inheritance off from the rear of your Mercedes.

The Lottery Mentality

People with the "Lottery Mentality" believe that their lucky break is just around the corner. When they finally hit the jackpot, it is going to be well worth the wait. They want just one more roll of the dice. Just one more tussle with the one-armed bandit. They scratch, and they scratch, and they scratch, and they scratch one instant winner ticket after another. For them the jackpot is always just around the next corner.

They always feel their luck is about to change. However, as soon as they round the corner another curve lies ahead. They see other people who are successful and erroneously equate success with luck instead of hard work and preparation. To them, being "blessed" is a matter of luck.

They do not feel the need to plan, save or prepare for a rainy day. For this group everything is tomorrow. They sing of a better day coming tomorrow, bright sunshine and the whole nine yards.

Yes, they do occasionally bask in the sun. However, it is always short-lived, because they are forever in the pursuit of bigger and better jackpots and will risk all they have in pursuit of it.

Now, those of you who do not gamble do not start to feel "holier than thou". You have a similar mentality called "The Unnecessary Miracles Mentality".

The Unnecessary Miracles Mentality

For all of you Dear Brothers and Sisters who do not play the lottery, some of you still fall into what I call the "Unnecessary Miracles Mentality".

Just like the Lottery Mentality, you try to play God like a slot machine. Instead of cherries and fruit, your machine pulls down Malachi 3:8, or Psalms 37:25.

You are quick to say, "Chile, I pay my tithes. God will rebuke the devourer for my sake". Yes, you may have paid God his 10% but you were foolish and slothful with the 90%. You did not pay your rent, phone or light bill, but you paid Red Lobster, Macy's and the nail lady. You knew those tires were bald, but chose to buy a new dress for Women's Day.

You do not feel the need to prepare a budget or plan for the future. You quote portions of scripture that talk about how God looks after the lilies of the field or when David said that he never seen the righteous forsaken. However, when the eviction notice is slid under your door or when Bubba drives away with your new car, you start pulling on God similar to how the other people pull on the slot machine. "Come on Lord, come on." You begin rattling off scriptures and reminding God of what He did for Peter, or the woman with the little oil.

The truth is, you got yourself into this trouble by not planning or being frugal with your 90%. Just as the person with the lottery mentality plans his life around an unexpected windfall, you live your life haphazardly and without care for tomorrow trusting God for an unnecessary miracle.

Yes, God is a miracle working God, but come on now, He made the provision for you to pay your light bill, but you chose that new suit instead. Well, my Brothers and Sisters, I know you gave your tithes, but instead of God dazzling you with an unnecessary miracle, He may choose to pull you closer to him. You just might find yourself all dressed up in your new suit in an intimate setting with God, reading your scriptures by candlelight.

The "I Can Change 'Em Mentality"

Have you ever met someone and realized that despite all the reasons you enjoy their company there are some definite characteristics that just plain annoy you? Do not fall in the mentality that believes you can change a person. Be it a friend or a mate, you cannot change anyone, only God can.

You can work on yourself and pull yourself up by your bootstraps, but you cannot pull someone else against their will or to a point beyond their potential

Remember, you are moving out from stagnant, destructive and barren places in **your** life. When you move out, it may leave some folk behind. Work on you and let God change them.

It's Over for Here!

Chapter

Three

Ten Things God Can't Stand...

3

Ten Things God Can't Stand…

1. Stealing His Money

Five, ten, fifteen, twenty… Just like a little child's game some times even mature Christians try to play games with God. He called for the tithes to be 10% not 5% or even less when things are not going well. We play catch up when it is convenient for us or when the devourer has put enough lumps on our head. Even after all of the games we play, we have the nerve to wonder why our blessings start playing hopscotch.

2. Slothfulness

We are the servants of the Most High God. Have you ever heard of a master that loved a lazy servant? No! The servant that gets the most perks is the one who has proven himself useful and always on top of his tasks. People who are lazy, do not see the benefit of the work to be done. They do not see the "big picture".

3. Being Unorganized.

Part of health is mental health. When your surroundings are unorganized, it drains your mental health whether you realize it or not. If your desk is a mess, how many extra minutes a day do you waste looking for things you need?

It's Over for Here!

Calculate that by weeks, months, or an entire career. We could easily assume one might waste an hour a day trying to find misplaced items at work or home.

Calculate one hour a day times 365 days in a year. What could you have accomplished with 365 more hours a year? Perhaps, some of those things you said you did not have time for. Multiply that times 20 years. Many a dying soul has tried to bargain with the death angel for just a little more time. On your dying bed, one more day would be appreciated, not to mention all the time we have actually wasted in our lifetime!

I once knew a person who was meticulously organized. The pots and pans in his home had one assigned place as did each plate and glass. I commented that this person must have been extremely energetic. He responded that no, actually it was the opposite. He assigned everything a specific place because he was too lazy to waste time looking for things all the time.

Each room in the house had everything he needed in that room. For example, the kitchen, bathroom or workroom all had a pair of scissors. There was no need to take the bathroom scissors into the kitchen or work room. Each room had scissors in it. Likewise, every room was adequately equipped with everything necessary for that room. With his system he never felt like he was cleaning up, just filing things away where they belonged.

This person always had plenty of time to pursue other interests, gardening, woodworking, church activities etc., all because he had his surroundings organized.

As a carpenter, he had specific toolboxes already stocked with the necessary tools for each type of job. He was undoubtedly one of the best handymen in town and his pay reflected it. Preparation and organization were his secret weapons.

This same philosophy followed through with his clothing, vehicles, finances and everything in his life. This person was not any smarter or more talented than anyone else, he had just tapped into one of life's great secrets: **God will not bless your mess!**

4. Whining

I am going to let you in on a secret: hush that whining! God is not moved by your whining. I used to think just like a child, Daddy loved me best. There was a time I just knew I was one of God's favorite kids. I thought He was blessing me more than average. As I matured from the Baby Saint stage to a more mature Saint, the blessings seemed to slow down. It seemed that I had to work at it with fasting, prayer and consecration.

When the blessings seemed to slow down, I thought that surely, if I cried and whined, God would let me have my way. WRONG! I thank God I was wrong. Most times, we do not even know what we need. God in his infinite wisdom knows what we need and when we need it. Somebody knew well and wrote a song that says, "You can't hurry God-you just have to wait".

We view the world from the time we got here through perhaps the threescore and ten years we might live. God's view encompasses all of eternity what has been, what is and what is yet to come. To God, a day is as 1,000 years and 1,000 years is as one day. Who are we to put Him on a schedule?

Life does bring about a change. I went from thinking I was one of God's favorite kids, to failing so many test, I felt like I was completing part of my spiritual journey on the short bus, (Special Ed for Stubborn Saints).

5. Being Unproductive

One of the famous parables in the Bible is the parable of the talents. In **Matthew 25:14-30** we see that God gave each of us talents according to our abilities. He expects that we produce.

> **Matthew 25:14-30**
> *For the kingdom of heaven is as a man traveling into a far country, who called his own servants, and delivered unto them his goods. 15. And unto one he gave five talents, to another two, and to another one; to every man according to his several ability; and straightway took his journey. 16. Then he that received the five talents went and traded with the same, and made them other five talents. 17. And likewise he that had received two, he also gained other two. 18. But he that had received one went and digged in the earth, and hid his lord's money. 19. After a long time the lord of those servants cometh, and reckoneth with them. 20. And so he that had received five talents came and brought other five talents, saying Lord, thou deliveredst unto me five talents; behold, I have gained besides them five talents more. 21. His lord said unto him, Well done, thou good and faithful servant; thou hast been faithful over a few things, I will make thee ruler over many things; enter thou into the joy of the lord. 22. He also that had received two talents came and said, Lord, thou deliveredst unto me two*

talents: behold, I have gained two other talents beside them. 23. His lord said unto him, Well done, good and faithful servant; thou hast been faithful over a few things, I will make thee ruler over many things: enter thou into the joy of thy lord. 24. Then he which had received the one talent came and said, Lord, I knew thee that thou art a hard man, reaping where thou hast not sown, and gathering where thou hast not strowed; 25. And I was afraid, and went and hid thy talent in the earth: lo, there thou hast that is thine. 26. His lord answered and said unto him, Thou wicked and slothful servant, thou knewest that I reap where I sowed not, and gather where I have not strowed: 27. Thou oughtest therefore to have put my money to the exchangers, and then at my coming I should have received mine own with usury. 28. Take therefore the talent from him, and give it unto him which hath ten talents. 29. For unto every one that hath shall be given, and he shall have abundance: but from him that hath not shall be taken away even that which he hath. 30. And cast ye the unprofitable servant into outer darkness: there shall be weeping and gnashing of teeth.

Well my friends take a lesson from this parable. Dig up that talent and put it to work!

Another scripture talks about bearing fruit.

John 15:1-8
I am the true vine, and my Father is the husbandman. 2. Every branch in me that beareth not fruit he taketh away: and every branch that beareth fruit he purgeth it, that it may bring forth

more fruit. 3. Now ye are clean through the word which I have spoken unto you. 4. Abide in me, and I in you. As the branch cannot bear fruit of itself except it abide in the vine; no more can ye, except ye abide in me. 5. I am the vine, ye are the branches: He that abideth in me and I in him, the same bringeth forth much fruit; for without me ye can do nothing. **6. If a man abide not in me, he is cast forth as a branch, and is withered; and men gather them, and cast them into the fire, and they are burned.** *7. If ye abide in me, and my words abide in you, ye shall ask what ye will, and it shall be done unto you. 8. Herein is my Father glorified, that ye bear much fruit; so shall ye be my disciples.*

Take special notice of verse number 6. When we are not producing, (no fruit) could it be because we have fallen away from God's will for our lives? Could it be that when people do not see us operating within our God given purpose and producing, they only see us withered and worn and have no use or respect for us? Yes, you are still going to Church, singing in the Choir, ushering and paying tithes. However, you are not walking in all that God has ordained for your life. You are not living up to the potential God has for you. You are not producing fruit!

Quite often when people disrespect you, it is because they see no fruit. The scripture says that men will gather them and cast them into the fire. Read those verses again and see how it all fits in. No Christ, no fruit, no fruit you get burned!

(When you are producing fruit, you will have others who are wasteful and lazy looking for you to provide for them.

They smoke, gamble and eat up their harvest, do not allow them to waste any of yours.)

6. Lack of Focus

To focus is to pull something into view. With a camera, unless you bring the tree you are trying to picture into focus, you may get a picture of the sky, a house or your thumb. Yes, there are many other things around the tree, but to get a picture of the tree, the camera has to be in focus.

We must keep our eyes on the prize as well; eternal life being the first and foremost. But in the here and now, we were created with a purpose, for a purpose. Within that purpose, we were created to enjoy life and be a joy to others. A lack of focus causes us to wander aimlessly through life. We miss out on many experiences and joys God intended for us to enjoy.

7. Excuses

God promised to never put on us more than we can bear. To make an excuse would be like saying, "God I don't think you got this one right. You knew I was going to have this wife and that we would be poor, or that I would have a mean boss on my job. So if you think I can set up a youth group for inner city kids, you didn't calculate all of the facts." Would you dare say that to God? Well, each time you make an excuse in essence that is what you are saying. Why would a kind and loving God create us for a purpose we were not capable of fulfilling?

It's Over for Here!

Jeremiah 29:11
*For I know the thoughts that I think toward you,
saith the Lord, thoughts of peace, and not of evil,
to give you an expected end.*

Don't you think the Creator knows the capabilities of the
creation more than the created does? Can you imagine a
piece of material the Wright Brothers used in their new
flying machine, telling them, "Hey what are you doing?
It is not possible to fly! And if it was, you certainly can't
use me, I've been cast aside, I was a reject back at the
plant." Do you get the picture? The Creator is wiser than
the creation and knows the creation's capabilities.

8. Envy

Envy, can be viewed as a lack of focus. You spend so
much time looking at what someone else has you will
eventually lose focus on what you can have if you put the
time and energy forth. Do not envy the Jones' new home.
You do not know the weekends they chose to forego
movies and other entertainment to save for their new
home. Perhaps Mrs. Jones did her own hair and nails for
2 years. Spend your time setting goals for yourself. Envy
is a waste of time and a sin.

Proverbs 14:30
*A sound heart is the life of the flesh: but envy the
rottenness of the bones.*

9. Deceit

Lying, stealing and evil plans have no part in God's army.
God says a liar will not even tarry in his sight. Do not
think you can expect a blessing from God utilizing these
tactics. Momentary gain obtained through evil practices

will not last. When you decide to cheat on taxes, job applications, credit applications or steal someone else's spouse, property or possessions, etc., you stop God's blessings.

Proverbs 37 1:2
Fret not thyself because of evildoers, neither be thou envious against the workers on iniquity. 2. For they shall soon be cut down like the grass, and wither as the green herb.

When we attempt to use deceit to get things we want, we are in essence telling God, I do not trust you to take care of me so I am going to do it my way. What an insult to the Father!

10. Mediocrity

God is a God of excellence! Look in the Bible. Look at the elaborate detail He required in the building of the Ark of the Covenant, Noah's Ark and Solomon's Temple just to name a few. Look at all of His creations. Look at the human body. The intricate details involved in a simple strand of hair. The Scriptures declare that we are fearfully and wonderfully made. God expects the creatures that He took so much time and care to create to do the same.

Have you ever met a person who took even the smallest task and made a masterpiece? A great cook can make a pot of pinto beans taste like a feast. God loathes mediocrity! Mediocrity is lukewarm. We must endeavor to put our best foot forward at all times. Someone once said, "If it is worth doing, it is worth doing well."

It's Over for Here!

One important fact about the "Ten Things God Can't Stand", is that if you are guilty on one, watch out, they are like little monsters, they run in packs. If you allow one in, he will bring his friends. You must continually do a self-check on the "Ten Things God Can't Stand" throughout your lifestyle "remix" process.

The good news is God wants to help you. He wants you to succeed so much that even before you were born, he put inside of you everything it took to lead a prosperous and successful life. It is unfortunate that some of us have to go around and around only to realize the answers were always right in front of us.

Anything worthwhile is HARD! Let no one fool you. As with work done well, the pay is rewarding. There are so many things in life for you to enjoy, but you have been limiting yourself by self-defeating behaviors. It is time to wake up and live! Once you take your head out of the sand and take a good look around, the unknown fear is not as frightening. The truth is, all the time your head was in the sand, your behind was taking a beating in plain view for everyone to see. (Besides the other obvious benefits of changing stances, your sun-baked weather beaten derriere will thank you.)

It's Over for Here!

It's Over for Here!

Chapter

Four

Pull the Boogey Man Out

4

Pull the Boogey Man Out

Why do we hide from our problems? The strange part about it is the longer we hide, the bigger our imagination makes the monster out to be. What started out as a bed mite ends up being a twenty story high, four-eyed monster terrorizing our world crushing everything in its way.

Fear and imagination are a powerful combination. I remember when my oldest grandson was four. The first time he spent the night at my new house, I tucked him into the guest bedroom. We said our goodnights and I went across the hall to my room.

Everything was fine for about five minutes, when he ran frantically into the room. "What's wrong, I asked?" I reassured him that there was nothing to be afraid of and encouraged him to try again.

I tucked him in again. Once again, everything was fine for about five minutes. This time I figured I would be smarter than a four year old. I told him that Jesus was with him and that he could imagine that Jesus was sitting in that nice blue chair in his room. He agreed and I went back to bed.

Five minutes passed; no problem. Ten minutes passed, still no problem. All of a sudden, he came running as though the house was on fire. I asked, "DeAaron, what is wrong?" His sincere and earnest reply was, "Jesus went downstairs".

It's Over for Here!

I did not know what to say after that. I quietly walked across the hall and slept in the nice blue chair until he fell asleep. It was hard to argue with the boy. When Jesus leaves, it is definitely time to go.

We find that even as adults, fear and imagination keep a lot of us afraid of the boogey man. Have you ever thought you saw something moving in your room at night, only to find at daylight that it was a shadow of a shirt or something? It is funny how once you expose something the terror diminishes.

What kind of fears do grown folk have? Some fear rejection, others failure. They ask themselves, "What if I don't get that promotion? Or what if I get the promotion and fail?" They may fear humiliation and say to themselves, "If I fail what if they ridicule me?"

"What if"...two powerful words that precede events that almost never happen!

What does fear do? Fear immobilizes us, keeps us from moving forward. Where do fears come from, experiences of the past, bad memories? One might say, "I remember the time they laughed when I gave the wrong answer." "I remember the time I almost got in an accident, so I don't want to drive a car anymore." Fear can keep us trapped within set parameters, afraid to venture out. Fear is also like a muscle, the more we use it the stronger it gets. Most fears are not even based on actual experiences, but our perception of what could happen. For the most
part, we need to treat fear like ketchup on a duck's back. It will eventually go away as long as we keep pushing forward.

It's Over for Here!

Chapter Five

Mirror, Mirror on the Wall

5

MIRROR, MIRROR ON THE WALL

Tammy and Greg found themselves in a heck of a predicament. Tammy blamed Greg and of course, Greg blamed Tammy. Spring according to the calendar was 10 days away. This newlywed couple had just survived their second winter together. According to Tammy, this winter was their first and last without heat. It seemed like every time they went to pay on bills other emergencies arose. For example, the time Greg's car was stolen. It was found later, damaged and needed repair. The insurance deductible was too high to be of any benefit. As an outside salesman, with no car Greg had no check. Tammy's car had died months earlier. The mere sum of $850.00 never seemed to materialize. There was always some shut-off notice or immediate need grabbing for the money.

Greg was not a tither at all. He would argue that if God wanted him to pay tithes, He would have given him more money. Tammy often found herself using her tithes to bail out Greg. When he was working, he never had gas to get to work. Tammy would give him gas money just to get him out of the house. She worked from home and enjoyed her peace and quiet. She always somehow caught up on her tithes, but it still threw everything off.

It's Over for Here!

Somehow, the two had survived the entire winter with electric heaters and blankets. Months had passed and not one dime had been paid on the $1,500.00 gas bill. With the extra pull of electricity from the heaters running all winter, the electric bill was now $1,500.00 as well. (They should have at least anticipated a higher electric bill and paid extra on it.)

What went wrong? It seems that in 9 months something could have been paid on the bill.

Tammy blamed Greg's lottery habit. Once he won $1,200.00. Her requests to pay on the bill fell on deaf ears. Greg felt that God was trying to bless him and 3 days later the lottery had all of the money right back. There was still no heat in the house.

They most recently had started putting their money together and seemed to make some strides. The dental insurance was reinstated. Both car insurances were paid in full. The internet service was back on and arrangements were made for the delinquent cable bill.

Tammy's home business had picked up with some new clients. However, this was offset by the old clients who were upset because they could no longer receive free or reduced rate services. According to Greg, this was Tammy's major downfall.

Now, in the mail, 3 delinquent bills had resurrected and were now seeking to collect again. The mailbox was full and the phones were ringing off the hook again.

The truth is Tammy and Greg both in their mid 40's, met and married a little over 2 years ago, but this scenario is not unfamiliar to either of them. They had multiple bankruptcies, repossessions, foreclosures, evictions and closed bank accounts between them. Different people same stories.

The things Greg told Tammy about herself were hurtful but true. She spent years working for a social services agency where services were free or reduced to clients. She ran her business like a social club or a missionary society. She did good work, but seemed to be more impressed with clients praising her work or rescuing a business out of a crisis than making good money. Clients took Tammy's kindness for weakness. They would pay the deposit, but months would pass before she would receive any of the balance.

At any point, she would have hundreds of dollars owed to her, yet, her business phone service would get disconnected for $150.00.

Her clients would even tell her that they had other bills to pay. They teased and said surely with the quality of her work she had more money than they did. They agreed to pay her as soon as things got better for them.

Because she worked so hard and received her pay in dribbles, she became discouraged and refused to seek out new clients.

The majority of her clients were now her friends. Tammy was not able to separate her business affairs from her personal. She made friends very quickly. Greg was right. She did run her business like a local charity. Her clients prospered and grew from her advice. They drove nice cars, while she continued to ride the bus. They had heat, hot water and cooking facilities.

It's Over for Here!

During the time they were without cooking facilities, Tammy and Greg found a quaint little restaurant where they could eat out five or six days a week for $12.00 per day.

Tammy blamed Greg's smoking and gambling for their financial crisis. According to Tammy, being a commissioned salesman was no way to make a living. Greg was in a comfort zone. He carried around a check from ten years ago when he made good money. The truth is that with the internet, the industry had changed drastically. Even factoring for inflation, he now made less than he did ten years ago; not to mention the rising cost of gas.

Greg was constantly whining and complaining about his job, at least six hours of his eight hour day. He considered himself a "Baby Saint", he had only been saved, (on paper) for two years. Faith for him meant trusting God for the number.

Although the couple felt things had never been worse for either of them, they blamed it on the economy and each other. Everyone they knew was hitting it hard. (Perhaps they never heard the saying birds of a feather.)

Greg and Tammy became experts at the blame game as they steadily sank further and further into debt. They each could accurately diagnose the others problems. However, the truth of the matter is that the other person is usually never the problem. The problem is usually the head in the mirror!

Get the mote out of your own eye first. Stop blaming others.

It's Over for Here!

The Blame Game

All too often, we find ourselves saying, "I would have been successful if it had not been for... Well today is the last day you should allow yourself to play the Blame Game. Scripture tells us, "You ran well but who did hinder you?" Some of you blame other people such as spouses, old boyfriends, employers, your elementary school classmates, your Pastor and any number of other people.

 Some of you blame circumstances such as being born on the wrong side of the tracks. Who declared what side of the tracks was wrong? Well whatever the excuse is, here is your chance to place the blame.

List twenty people, places or things that you feel have held you back from being successful.
Now, look at those lame excuses.

You might argue that some of them are legitimate excuses. Perhaps one of your excuses was that you were born blind, or lame. Other excuses you might use could be that you were abused as a child or your parents left you. Perhaps you were poor and could not go to school.

Well, I still call them lame because when God created you He equipped you with everything it took to be successful in the life and purpose He created you for.

Where we often go wrong is when we compare someone else's life and successes to what we wish ours would be. The scriptures tell us "that we are fearfully and wonderfully made." It all also tells us that we can do all things through Christ that strengthens us. Philippians 4:13.

Think back on stories you have heard of people who overcame tremendous odds to achieve greatness. Story after story, you hear of how they rose from poverty and obscurity to a place of prominence. What they lacked in finances, physical ability or acceptance, they made up for with dogged determination, passion and a plan.

So, back to your excuses, put them to rest once and for all. Yes, we have challenges in life, but nothing to the caliber that can prevent us from accomplishing that which God created us for. We were all born with more creative juices than we can use in 5 lifetimes!

Now, go back to the Blame List. Take each item listed and carefully evaluate it. Perhaps one of your excuses was, "I would do better in business if my clients would pay me on time". It does not make sense for you to blame the clients for your predicament. You are the one who needs to stop rendering services on credit!

If you follow your gut feeling, you can usually weed out problems in the beginning. It has happened over and over again. Stop falling for it. You usually feel uncomfortable in the beginning. You know who is going to be a problem child. You usually receive your biggest headaches from the clients you bent over backwards to accommodate. They wanted special discounts or they never provided the information requested on time. Well you certainly cannot lay the blame on them when you could have avoided getting yourself in the same situation again.

The Shame Game

Similar to the Blame Game is the Shame Game. Perhaps you are ashamed (or embarrassed), of your weight, speech, writing abilities, or some other aspect of your life. It might be you have a child or children out of wedlock, have been married 4 times, lost your job, owe everybody in town money, or have been to jail. Again, list up to 10 things you are ashamed or embarrassed about.

Now, go back over the list. If it is something you did that you are ashamed of, if you have not already, ask God for forgiveness.

Micah 7:19 He will again have compassion on us, and will subdue our iniquities. You will cast all our sins into the depths of the sea."

Once God forgives, He throws it into the sea of forgetfulness and remembers it no more.

Now, go to the restroom or any place you have a mirror and a sink. Fill up a glass of water for each thing that is causing you to feel ashamed. Look yourself in the mirror. Just like you asked God to forgive you, ask yourself and forgive yourself.

Now take each glass of water and speak out the shame it represents. Pour the entire glass of water down the drain. Imagine it flowing down the drain, out to your sewer system all through town and out to the sea. Yes, the same sea God has cast it into. Tell the devil, "I will be tormented no more! I have been forgiven and have forgiven myself. Poof, be gone."

It's Over for Here!

Isaiah 1:18
Come now, and let us reason together, says the Lord, though your sins are like scarlet, they shall be as white as snow; though they are red like crimson, they shall be as wool."

Continue until the contents of all of the glasses are down the drain. For added measure, rinse them well, so your imagination cannot tell you there are traces of anything left. If you pour a glass of water in the sea, is there anyway you can go back and scoop up that exact glass of water? Well, anytime the devil tries to bring back those old hurts and shames, realize he cannot do it. God has forgiven you, end of story. It is up to you to walk in that forgiveness, move forward, not side stepping, or back tracking. Always remember this visual exercise. Shame and guilt are down the drain!

The mind and the imagination are powerful tools! Keep in mind that shame and embarrassment are relatives of fear. God does not give us a spirit of fear. So where does it come from? You, and the devil.

Your mind can conjure up false things to the point that they appear real. Get rid of all those boogey men in your closet. They are not real. They do not exist. Shame and embarrassment are not real. Think about it, no one can make you ashamed or embarrassed, you allow it by choosing to be ashamed or embarrassed over a situation. Thank God, you have chosen to wash all of that foolishness down the drain.

A word of caution: This is not an excuse for you to go out, party hearty and try to wash it down the drain Sunday morning before you march down the aisle to the choir stand or your Usher post. Remember asking God to forgive you was the first step. You must truly repent (turn around) with no desire or intention to repeat like behavior. Delete repeat!

If you are a single parent, you owe it to yourself to move on with your life. Others do not have to understand how you can walk with your head high. That is between you and God. If it is God's will, in His time He will send you a good mate.

Just because you have a child or two out of wedlock doesn't mean you have to settle for less. Do not waste your precious time kissing frogs. Love and take care of your babies and when you are ready-if it is God's will. He will send your Boaz. Believe me, you do not want to rush God. Let God get through with him. We hear the phrase, "Please be patient with me God is not through with me yet". Definitely when it comes to a mate, you had better wait until God is through with them and the dust has settled.

Back to Greg and Tammy, if you were to inspect each of their lives prior to them marrying each other, there were many issues of unresolved blame and shame for past financial mistakes, and life choices. To admit that perhaps their lives could stand some tweaking would be to admit past mistakes. Talk about pride! What does the Bible say about pride?

> **Proverbs 16:28**
> *Pride goeth before destruction and a haughty spirit before a fall.*

When pride keeps us from taking a stark look in the mirror and making the necessary adjustments, destruction

It's Over for Here!

is sure to follow.   They chose to hide their heads out of shame and blame hoping this too will pass.

A final word on shame:

> ***Philippians 3:13***
> *Brethren, I count not myself to have apprehended: but this one thing I do, forgetting those things which are behind, and reaching forth unto those things which are before.   14. I press toward the mark for the prize of the high calling of God in Christ Jesus.*

What was Paul really saying? Brother I am not there yet either, but I know one thing, I am going to work what I have, to get what I want through the authority Christ has given me to do so.

Jesus bore our sins and shame on the cross on Calvary, leave them up there and keep on pressing forward!

It's Over for Here!

It's Over for Here!

Chapter Six

Move Two Feet

6

Move Two Feet

When we experience the death of a loved one, we experience some very stressful and changing times. I remember when my husband died. It started out a beautiful September afternoon. After church, I laid down to take a nap. All of a sudden, I heard him scream and I went downstairs. He was pacing frantically back and forth. He looked bewildered like a deer struck by the lights of a car. I rushed him to the emergency room.

After arriving at the hospital, he had come to himself and we began to talk. Little did either of us know that he would never return home. They found a blockage in his artery and scheduled surgery. On the operating table, he suffered a massive stroke and was in a coma for three months before he died.

We had been married a little over a year. We had delayed making and updating our Wills and other legal documents. Ironically, we had an appointment with an attorney a week later.

My husband was thirty years my senior and had children older than I was. I was self-employed at the time. During the three months he was in the hospital and eventually the nursing home, I lost all of my clients.

Because of the short time, we were married and my age, I was not entitled to any benefits as a surviving spouse.

It's Over for Here!

The insurance policy was still in his ex-wife's name even though she had agreed and signed off of all insurance policies in the divorce papers years ago. For the insurance company's protection she had to sign a document confirming that she had signed the divorce documents and was aware of the language regarding the insurance.

To make a long story short, she refused and they had to pay the insurance proceeds to her as the wife. As for the funeral expenses, she was not obligated to pay because she was not his wife.

O.K. now, here I was, self-employed with no clients, a hefty mortgage and a $10,000.00 funeral bill. The court eventually decided that they would split the insurance with the ex-wife receiving the larger portion. However, the insurance policy had diminished considerably because he had recently turned seventy years old.

On Valentine's Day of the following year, (three months after he passed) the pressure had really gotten to me. I was determined to drive out to the graveyard and let him know how everybody was treating me and all of the problems I had.

(Did I forget to mention that when my husband died on a Saturday morning, that my father passed two days later?)

I had reached my limit. I drove out to the cemetery, sobbing profusely all the way. Once I got there and came to where his plot was, I realized that he was not even there! There was nothing there but cold dirt and dead flowers! I came back to my senses. I guess the good cry helped.

It's Over for Here!

Well, mission accomplished, at least I felt better. I got back into my car and drove towards the gate. I had only been in there ten or fifteen minutes, but by that time, it had gotten dark, very dark. Worse than that, they had closed the gate and locked me in the cemetery, me and about five thousand dead folks!

Talk about having a bad day, this takes the cake. I immediately started thinking o.k. God is trying to teach me something. Let me learn it fast. As long as it is not an "Ezekiel in the Valley of the Dry Bones" experience, I was ready to learn it and get out of there.

I got out of the car and tried to see if I could find a lock release or even pick the lock. No, this was definitely one of those Bible gates, steadfast and unmovable.

Not having too many athletic days in my life, climbing the fence was a short fleeting thought, very short; especially considering the six inches of spikes that rest atop each fence pole. I thought of several cartoon scenes of being found in the morning impaled by a wrought iron fence trying to get out of the cemetery in a fur coat. I could imagine the guard in the morning, "Hey Charlie, call Animal Services, I think we found Big Foot". It was not funny at the time.

I had tried going to the left, no success, then to the right, still no luck and going back was not an option. It was really, truly dark by now.

After getting back in the car I began honking the horn and flashing my lights. Then fear gripped me by the throat and reminded me of my predicament. I was safer inside in my car. It was foolish to advertise that I was here alone, in the middle of nowhere. The known fear suddenly became more appealing than the unknown.

I started assessing the total situation. Maybe God wanted me to sit inside the gate to realize that my problems out there were not as bad as I thought. Yes, I could sell my house, I could get a job, I could just start over. Plenty of people have started over.

As I sat trying to figure out what I was supposed to figure out, it dawned on me that I had a prepaid cell phone. I only had three minutes on it for an emergency. If this did not qualify as an emergency, I don't know what would.

I dialed 9-1-1. After the lady stopped laughing, she told me not to go anywhere and that she would see what she could do.

She told me to call her back at 3:00 a.m. It was now about 8:00 p.m. Well, that did not work, but at least the 9-1-1 call was free.

I asked myself, which one of my friends would I be able to reach at home without a child picking up the phone wasting my three minutes. I needed to get an adult quickly and explain my dilemma before the phone shut off.

It was definitely Carol. The conversation went like this, "Hi, Carol, this is Debbie. This is not a joke. I am locked in the cemetery where Roosevelt is and I need you to get me out!" At that moment, the phone went CLICK!

Oh well, I don't think she got all of that. What do I do now Lord? Maybe I am supposed to count my blessings. Well I got a full tank of gas and a new gospel c.d. No, on second thought, this could not be what God wants me to do trapped in a cemetery in the middle of nowhere.

Maybe He wants to make me learn to fight, and keep seeking and not give up so fast.

Could it be He wants me to praise Him in this situation? I started having my own praise and worship service in the dark, dark cemetery, in the middle of nowhere. I thought about Paul and Silas locked up in the jail singing. I really did start feeling better. I was prepared to sing until 7:00 a.m. I definitely was not in the mood to sleep.

In the midst of praising God, a car drove up on the other side of the fence. A little lady got out of the car, which was a surprise. I wanted somebody with some muscles. Here I was in the need of some serious rescue and out comes a little old lady. At that point, I could not complain, I was the one who managed to get locked up in the cemetery.

I jumped out of the car and ran to the gate. The lady said "Ma'am, get back in your car and move two feet."

I thought to myself, what kind of nonsense was this? I am not rolling my brand new Cadillac up to a gate to stand up on it and climb out. I wondered to myself, where is your key? I followed her instructions anyway. I carefully rolled my car two feet from the exit and the huge iron gate began to slowly roll to the side.

I was shocked. The truth was she could not get me out of there; I was the only one who could. There was no big long key or secret code. All I had to do was move forward. I instantly got the message God was trying to give me. In life all that counts is moving forward. Just

It's Over for Here!

like in the cemetery, I went to the left to look for an escape, no success. Then I went to the right looking for an escape and was still stranded. I did not even try to go backwards. I knew there was nothing there but cold dirt and dead flowers. Our past is the same way.

In life, we are going to have problems, many of them, ask Job. We can assess a situation, look for assistance, seek answers, but the only thing that matters is moving forward. I thought that perhaps the gate swung out or swung in. I was more concerned about damaging my car if the gate swung in. From my frazzled perspective, my car was a way out of my financial troubles. I could sell it and get some breathing room. I was not about to jeopardize that option.

I had tried every direction but forward based upon my limited information. Isn't that just how life is? We have limited information. Moving forward requires faith. Having faith, is not understanding how the gate works, but knowing that your deliverance is in moving forward.

I used to hear the old Saints say, "If you make one step God will make two". Isn't it beautiful that God knows every detail of the trauma you are going through? He didn't ask you to move the first eight blocks, just two feet. The woman told me to move two feet. My deliverance was only two feet away. It did not make sense to me, but it worked! I was the one who had to make the next move.

By the way, Carol showed up a few minutes later. My hero! (And you wonder why she is one of my best friends for life!) If the caretaker had not gotten there, I do not know what she would have done, but I would have been Paul and she would have been Silas until the gatekeeper came in. Thank God for good friends.

It's Over for Here!

It's Over for Here!

Section II
...And Move Forward!

Chapter
Seven

Ten Steps Out of a Rut

7

Ten Steps Out Of a Rut

Fortunately, God does not always make such dramatic illustrations. It took moving forward to get out of the predicament in the cemetery. Sometimes in life, we find ourselves stuck. Below is a list of ten steps to help you get out of a rut.

1. **Acknowledge that a crisis exists.**

_____

_____

_____

_____

2. **Define the crisis. What is actually happening now?**

_____

_____

_____

_____

3. **Identify the worst case scenario. What are your fears?**

_____

_____

_____

_____

_____

4. **Identify a best-case scenario.**

_____

_____

_____

_____

_____

It's Over for Here!

_____

_____

5. List all of the possible solutions and outcomes.

_____

_____

_____

_____

_____

6. Identify resources needed for each possible solution to work.

_____

_____

_____

_____

_____

_____

_____

_____

7. **Identify people needed to help you**.

_____

_____

_____

_____

_____

_____

8. **Pick one or two strategies to work on, Plan A and Plan B.**

_____

_____

_____

_____

9. Lay out steps and proceed.

_____

_____

_____

_____

_____

10. Accept the facts and acknowledge the fact that this crisis will pass; although the outcome may be quite different than you had expected. Celebrate and resolve that God's will be done.

_____

_____

_____

_____

You should not fret too much about being able to come with the perfect plan. Remember, the only thing that matters is moving forward. God is going to bless your efforts and meet you at the gate. Your deliverance is only a short distance away, but you have to have the faith to move forward.

Chapter Eight

Digging Out With a Teaspoon

8

Digging Out With a Teaspoon

Move just two feet. What an unbelievably short distance! That is how God is. He never requires too much of us. We are the ones so hard on ourselves. You may want to lose fifty pounds. You starve and deprive yourself to the point that you just give up. Yes, you may have lost seventeen pounds but that was so hard you lost interest in trying to lose the rest.

If you talk to someone who has lost weight and kept it off for years, I would bet they lost it in smaller increments over a longer period of time. It was not a quick fix diet but rather a lifestyle change.

You may not be willing to starve and run twenty miles to loose five pounds a week, but you can give up some of your sweets or stop eating after 8:00 p.m. You can also commit to a smaller goal such as walking ten minutes, five days a week and drinking eight glasses of water. Most of us can. You will find that the ten minutes will eventually become a habit and you will find yourself walking thirty minutes or more before you know it.

What are some of your goals? Can they be broken down into smaller increments? They probably can. I understand you want to get your Ph.D., but concentrate on your G.E.D. first. Celebrate that victory and then move on up to your Associates degree and from there on up the ladder. You might say, with the job and responsibilities I have, it will take me twenty years. Well, if you do not pursue your dream now, what is going to happen in twenty years? You will be twenty years older still dreaming.

> **Joel 2:28**
> *And it shall come to pass afterward, that I will pour out my spirit upon all flesh; and your sons and your daughters shall prophesy, your old men shall dream dreams, your young men shall see visions.*

The scripture says that the old men shall dream dreams and the young men shall see visions. (The Wright interpretation: You had better get with the vision while you are young or when you get old, it may be nothing but a dream.)

Let's suppose one of your goals was to save $1,000.00. Can you save $20.00 a week for one year? No? How about give up your pedicures and manicures for a year and save $7.69 a week? Does that sound better? No? You can think about taking your lunch to work 4 days a week. Well, you get the picture. You can save $1,000.00. The more committed you are the faster you will reach your goal.

The same philosophy holds true for any goal. Baby steps can render giant rewards. Success and accomplishment are addictive. Develop an achiever's attitude.

> **Philippians 4:13**
> *I can do all things through Christ which strengtheneth me.*

(Wright Interpretation: "God's got my back and I and I am going to push forward!)

It's Over for Here!

Break your dreams into smaller goals and celebrate as you achieve each milestone. You will save yourself a lot of grief and stress.

Greg and Tammy in an earlier chapter could have put small amounts aside to pay the gas bill. A whole year went by with struggling and trying to adapt, yet not one dime had been paid on the bill. They had pity parties and blamed everyone and everything else except the man in the mirror. Their way of adapting to their "misfortune" was to eat out every day instead of sacrificing and getting the gas turned back on. Neither one of them even thought of getting a part-time job and allocating the extra income towards the bill. They suffered from many of the mentalities listed in this book. The "Junebugs" in the family always had their utilities turned off. Why should they expect any different. Most folks they knew were going through the same thing. The "Junebug's" felt that if they could just hit one good number, their worries would be over.

You can faithfully pay your tithes, give your offerings and say to yourself, God will do the rest. That is not enough. You still have to be a good steward of the 90% you have left.

All of the excuses we make are the result of warped thinking and mentalities. God is the only one who can overcome such mentalities, but we do have a part to play.

Life is truly a journey. It really does not matter whether you are in a Hoopty or a Hummer, keep rolling. Sometimes on life's journey, we may find ourselves singing, "Row, row, row your boat gently down the stream, merrily, merrily, merrily, merrily, life is but a

It's Over for Here!

dream". We are laid back and secure. On other times, it is more like, "Jack be nimble, Jack be quick, Jack jump over the candlestick". We find ourselves leaping over one fire after another. But then there are the times when we are like Humpty Dumpty, everything crashes at our feet and all of the kings horses and all of the king's men, can't put what has fallen back together again. Oh, but let me encourage you--the King of Glory can!

It's Over for Here!

Chapter Nine

Weathering a Sudden Storm

Weathering a Sudden Storm

One of life's certainties is that life is uncertain. When you least expect it, a storm arises. Something happens in your life to knock you flat on your back. Sometimes you can see it coming just like a natural storm you can feel it brewing for hours or even days. Other times, it appears suddenly out of a clear blue sky.

A storm can be anything from sudden sickness, death of a loved one, financial disaster or any number of unexpected occurrences. Regardless of any emergency preparations you may have, a storm can catch you off guard and makes you feel unsafe and for the moment take your focus off of everything else.

At our ages, most of us know all of the rules and procedures for weathering a natural storm, but here are some tips for weathering a spiritual storm.

1. **Seek Shelter**. The Word of God is a shelter in time of storm. God's Word has advice for everything we could possibly face in this life. At times, even as a seasoned Christian we need to go back to the basics. It is easy to counsel someone else facing marital problems. However, when the shoe is on our foot, we might get a different interpretation.

2. **Assume a low-lying position.** Hunker down against the storm. Assume a low-lying position such as prayer. In today's society we have become so accustomed to lightning fast, microwave speed satisfaction. If you would ask Abraham, Noah and Moses, I am sure they would be quick to tell you that God takes His time, and no amount of whining and crying is going to change His time. Somebody wrote a song that says, "You can't hurry God, you just have to wait….He may not come when you want him but He is right on time". While you are waiting on the Lord, keep a safe distance from doubters, discouragers and assume position until it is safe and all signs of the storm have succeeded. In the natural what happens in storms? The electric lines might be down—no lights. The phone lines may be down—no communication. When these things happen, we are warned to stay away from them. In the spiritual realm, it is the same. Stay away from people whose light has gone out or who have no communication with God. If they can't help themselves in a storm, they surely can't help you.

3. **Wait on the Son.** One thing that you can rest assured of is that eventually the SON will shine and you will feel His presence and reassurance that all is well! He even promised to wipe away all of your tears. Remember weeping may endure for a night, but joy comes in the morning! Praise God!

Action Steps: What are some positive things you can do while you are weathering a storm?

Suggestions:

- Help someone else who is in a storm.

- Keep a Praise Journal.

- Learn something new. It keeps your mind occupied while you are waiting out the storm.

God Won't Bless Your Mess

Sometimes what we think is a storm is of our own doing. God is a God of excellence and organization. Look at the examples in nature. Look at how beautiful and organized EVERYTHING He made is. Even a dandelion, which we consider a weed, has a beautiful yellow color and expertly detailed petals.

It is so important that we organize and beautify our surroundings. Since we are created in the image of God, shouldn't that mean that we innately love beauty and organization? Now, we may be too lazy to make our surroundings that way and make excuses. God blesses in an atmosphere of detail and organization. Look in the Bible, He even had the armies organize by certain groups and gave them specific detailed instructions.

When God moved on behalf of His people, it was usually organized and detailed. When He slew His enemies, He usually used confusion and disarray!

So, what does this mean? Make sure your storm is not of your own making by being unorganized and undisciplined. If you are operating a business and things are slow for you, look around you. Are there stacks of papers in each corner of the floor? Do you have a system to keep track of your projects? Are you constantly missing deadlines? Do you know how much money you owe or that is owed to you? If not, how do you think the Most Holy God we serve wants to come in the midst of that mess? The Angels that you have been calling to bring your blessings find themselves trying to tiptoe through your mess to get to you. Some of them refuse to come. They held their noses, covered their eyes and threw it in through the door. It's in there, but you can't find it under all that mess.

Clean it up, clean it up, clean it up! Being unorganized is a trick of the devil. He knows how God works. He also knows he cannot get you to outright, knowingly sin, but he can trap you up with clutter. Clutter around you eventually equates to clutter of the mind and can even make you depressed and sick physically. How can you excel in your purpose, confused and tired?

God loves us so much He will not even bless you because He knows you cannot handle any more than you already have on your plate. So to continue to pray for God to bless you while your surroundings are unorganized and in disarray, is praying amiss.

Instead of going on a fast, you need a shut-in. Shut yourself in your house with Mr. Clean, a vacuum cleaner and some trash bags.

After you conquer your home, do the office and every other area of your life. I promise you, you will come out of that shut-in, refreshed and revived, positioned to be blessed! Instead of your Angel of Blessing sitting at the curb, those dirt demons will be kicked to the curb. Do not let them back in!

It's Over for Here!

Organize everything you want God to bless. Clean out your purse. Take that rubber band off of your bulging wallet and clean and organize it. Get rid of clutter traps such as the "junk drawer". Organize everything you want God to bless and watch Him do it!

Chapter Ten

The Purpose of Pain

10

The Purpose of Pain

Pain lets you know something is happening. More specifically, something is wrong. It is a reminder and a warning. I have heard of people who refuse to take aspirin or painkiller until they have identified the source of the pain. They feel that if you mask the pain you miss what your body is trying to tell you. Aspirin does not necessarily cure the problem, but helps you cope with the pain.

Most of you have been feeling pain in areas of finance, health, relationships, career path or spiritually for some time now.

What is your pain trying to tell you? First, you have to identify what type of pain it is. Pain can be inflicted as punishment or pain can be part of a process like pruning. You could also have what we call growing pains. An athlete endures pain in pursuit of victory. They are willing to trade pain for victory. They often say no pain no gain.

A form of emotional and financial pain can come from your banking institution. Should you bounce a check, the NSF fee is designed to inflict pain. Pay bills late, the late fee is an example of pain. It is a fact that, pain in one area affects other areas. For example, you stump your toe, and your hand automatically comes to assist and support your hurt toe.

It's Over for Here!

What should you do when you experience pain? First, find out the source of your pain before you mask it or attempt to remedy the situation. If your foot was hurting, you wouldn't put an icepack on your head.

If the source of your pain is finances, spend time in that area. Study finance, go to some workshops and develop a strategy. If the source of your pain is career or spiritual, concentrate primarily on those areas. If you are truly determined that it's over for here, your pain has gotten to the level that you know exactly what ails you. A good starter's tip is since most of us fall short in more than one area, work the plans in this book in all areas of your life.

Remember, now when you move out, there is no looking back. I am sure you remember Lot's wife? Just like Lot and his family, God has prepared a way of escape for you. The pain you have been experiencing could simply be God's way of pruning you, preparing you or in some cases chastising you out of love.

A major source of pain is being out of the will of God as it relates to your purpose.

If God blessed you even though you were not fully walking within your purpose, most of you would be comfortable and content and never experience God's best for you.

I remember when my five year old grandson, James was acting up to the point he needed a spanking. I thought it appropriate to explain to him why I was spanking him. I knew he would not understand if I told him the Bible says that if we spare the rod, we spoil the child, so I tried to explain it so a 5 year old could understand. I told him that the Bible says the way to get the devil out of a child is to spank his behind in love. After the second swat on his bottom, he yelled out, "Stop, Grandma, don't get him out, leave him in there!" Some lessons in life hurt, but the ultimate goal is our growth. For little James' sake, I had to get him out!

When I think of the saying, "No pain, no gain", I am reminded of the little puzzle game you sometimes see in offices. It is one of those puzzles where you rock it back and forth to try to get the little ball through the hole to the next level. In our lives, storms and trials rock us to get us to the next level. We can resist and brace ourselves or we can try to make the best out of each storm and try to use it to move towards the hole, (goal).

At different levels of the puzzle, the ball drops easily to the next level. At other levels, it seems as though the game is over. No matter how you rock and shake the puzzle, the little ball just will not go through that little hole! At other times, it seems like it is a sure thing. The little ball hits the hole and bounces back out.

Even when that happens, do not despair. Always remember, whatever it looks like, whatever it feels like, our life (the puzzle) is in God's hands. His ultimate goal is that we grow and glow, moving to higher heights and deeper depths in Him.

So when things in your life start rocking, roll with it! It is God's desire that we move from glory to glory and level to level.

Chapter Eleven

The Countdown
What to do in the Next 90 Days

11

The Countdown…
What to Do in the Next 90 Days

Have you ever heard one of your favorite oldies but goodies, but it had a new twist to it? In the music world, the young people call it a "remix". The words are the same, but it has a different feel to it. There was nothing wrong with the other version, but the remix is more apropos for today's audience.

Our new lifestyle makeover can be viewed as a remix. You are still who you were before, just new and improved.

When you look at it, it is not the first time you got a new attitude. When you gave your life to Christ, you became a new creature, old things were passed away and all things became new.

II Corinthians 5:17
Therefore, if any man be in Christ, he is a new creature: old things are passed away; and all things are become new.

Some of you were truly blessed. When you got saved it happened all at once. Then again, some of you struggled awhile, flopping and bucking like a fish out of water, but you were eventually delivered, (or prayerfully in the process of being delivered).

It's Over for Here!

The Bible has several stories about people who went through lifestyle changes. We can look at the woman at the well or the account of Saul being transformed to Paul. The list of supernatural lifestyle remixes goes on and on. The Bible also talks about renewing our strength, and mounting up on wings of eagles.

Isaiah 40:31
But they that wait upon the Lord shall renew their strength; they shall mount up with wings as eagles; they shall run and not be weary; and they shall walk, and not faint.

Yes, it is possible for old dogs to learn new tricks! Yes, yes, yes, it is possible to maintain your new lifestyle makeover. The Word of God says:

III John 1:2
"Beloved I wish above all things that thou mayest prosper and be in health, even as thy soul prospereth.

Even though, this section is entitled, "The Countdown… What to do in the Next 90 Days", your transformation began when you picked up this book. Every step you make in the future can be ordered by the Lord to ensure your continued success.

What should you do today? A good place to start is with prayer. Write out your prayer to the Lord. Date it and keep it in the front of your journal. Refer to this prayer regularly.

The good part about this transformation is that you already have everything you need to start becoming who you were created to be.

It's Over for Here!

I remember once pulling out my tool drawer. Under the weight of all of the contents, the drawer fell to the ground. Out of frustration, I began to pick up the drawer and replace the items. There were so many tools in that drawer. I had even forgotten I had some of them. Some old, some new, but they were all good, useful tools. This is how our lives can be. We possess good attributes, gifts and talents, but they are unorganized like that tool drawer.

Look at the next 90 days as your time to organize your life and maximize the gifts and talents God has blessed you with.

A good place to start is with the basics. Keep in mind that these are minimums. You will need to adjust them according to your specific needs. A lot also depends on what region of the country you live in and your family's needs.

The Basics
Ten Things Grown Folk Ought to Have

1. **Pocket Money.** Grown men and women should make it their business to never allow themselves to get broke, busted or disgusted. Start with a simple $20.00 bill and $5.00 worth of change. Keep that bill in your wallet no matter what, for an emergency. Keep adding $20.00 bills until you have a comfortable amount depending upon where you live. If you need to catch a cab home in a major metropolitan city, you will need far more money than a small town in Kansas. A diet cola is not an emergency, but a taxi to the ATM is, if your car is stolen. Keep a small

amount of additional cash for your personal use, such as another $20.00. Keeping too much cash will tempt you to make impulse purchases and sabotage your new budgeting plans.

2. **Cookie Jar Money**. What would happen if a category 5 hurricane were predicted in your area and you had 45 minutes to get out of town? You would not be able to get to the ATMs because of the crowd. The $40.00 in your wallet will not get you a place to stay for the night or a warm meal. Perhaps you get a call that your child away at college was in a serious accident and need to rush to be by their side. You need some "Get Otta Dodge Money". One thing that is certain about emergencies, they do not wait until daylight. The amount you need depends on the climate you live in and the distance your loved ones are from you. There are certain areas of the country that are prone to certain types of emergencies, often giving rise to emergency evacuations. Prepare ahead for such emergencies. Grab your cookie jar and get outta Dodge!

3. **Keep a full tank of gas and dependable transportation**. Hey Cowboy, You can't get out of Dodge too fast on a hungry horse with a bum leg! Keep up on your vehicle maintenance such as oil changes and good tires. Change your prospective. Some people go through life seeing the glass half empty. The prosperity prospective sees it half full. A quarter tank of gas is a quarter tank of gas whether it is the quarter towards EMPTY or the quarter towards FULL. Make it a new rule to keep a full tank of gas. Fill up once

and each time you get down a ¼ tank---filler up. If you have a problem doing this, try placing tape at the mark ¼ down from full.   Do not ignore vehicle maintenance.   Make sure you have problems checked out early. A coat hanger is not a solution to a hanging muffler. Driving around with a case of Fix-A-Flat is no substitute for a good set of tires. Adding good oil to murky oil does not delay an oil change.   Place these maintenance items in your budget along with your car and insurance payments. Please do not forget the meter money. Keep some coins in the car. A couple of quarters can prevent a $15.00 parking ticket and a bench warrant should you forget to pay it.

4. **Keep $100.00 minimum in an ATM for smaller emergencies only**. Watch how few emergencies you have by truly planning better. Regular vehicle maintenance and organizing your finances can defray unnecessary emergency costs.

5. **Build up a $1,000.00 for a minimum emergency fund.** Keep a minimum of $1,000.00 in a savings account for an emergency. Build this account up to 6 months living expenses. If you need $5,000.00 per month to maintain your standard of living then multiply that by 6 for an emergency fund. Of course, this may take a while to accomplish, but the key word is BUILD. Brick by brick, dollar by dollar set a goal and push for it.

6. **Have basic insurances in place.** Life insurance, health insurance, auto, home, etc. Start out with at least the basics and work your way up

to the desired amounts over time. It is so embarrassing for families to have to raise money to bury a loved one who dies suddenly.

7. **Stock up on emergency rations.** Non-perishable food, clean water, medical supplies, batteries, candles, paper supplies, disinfectant, portable radio need to be readily available for emergencies. Also, remember to have an emergency kit in each vehicle as well as your home and office. Check with your local Red Cross for a complete listing of suggested items.

8. **Get your legal affairs in order**. Keep your Wills, Corporate documents, Birth Certificates, passports, account information, diplomas and certificates, burial plot information, address book with all important numbers in a safe place and a back-up copy somewhere else. Suppose your home is damaged by flood or fire, you need a second copy elsewhere.

9. **Keep a good basic business suit ready at all times**. Always keep a basic business suit including shoes and accessories ready for your big break. When your big break does come along, you want to look the part. Keep in mind that if you are an actor or a dancer your basic business suit may be a clown suit or a tutu. Whatever you require for your big break, is what you need to have ready when the opportunity comes knocking.

10. **Develop a personal mission statement and a life plan**. You can have every area of your life in meticulous order, but do you really

know why you are on this planet? What is your purpose? Take a good look at the obituaries. It is easy to tell who had goals in life and who just drifted wherever the wind took them. "Here lies Joe No Dream. He came, sucked air for 62 years and died." What did he deposit into the world for 62 years besides hot air? How did he make a difference to the world and the community around him? Was there anything in the world left better because he was here? Make your life count for something! Leave here with the world knowing you were here.

I am sure you are ready and equipped now to move forward. This section gives you some suggestions on how to move forward. Write your notes immediately following each section. Of course this book will not hold all of your notes, but it serves as a starting point. When you re-read this book a few months later, your notes will allow you to see progress.

Where do you start? Below is a suggested plan. Please customize your plan to reflect what you wish to accomplish. As hard as it is for some of us to believe, not everyone has a weight problem. Nor does everyone have a toxic relationship or financial chaos. You develop the plan to conquer those things that have been holding you back. But, for those who need a jump start, review the suggestions for Weeks One through Twelve. Your plan should be similar.

Let's Get Started!

Week One

Spend time in quiet meditation and prayer. Listen to what the Lord is saying to you. Do not rush into anything right now. Remember, you are going to delete the repeat button in your life. Settle down and listen. Any spiritual issues you have, ask for forgiveness and repent.

Adjust your attitude. Despite whatever is going on, see everything from an achiever's perspective. See ALL of your glasses as half-full and on the way to overflowing. Handle any immediate emergencies right away without delay, ie, a dangerous relationship, impending financial disaster or health issue.

Begin to take care of your body. Your body is the temple of the Holy Spirit. You probably already know everything you need to know to get started eating healthier and exercising your body. Start by including gentle stretching and walking in your daily routine. This has a dual benefit. Your body and spirit will benefit from good eating and exercise. Drink plenty of water! You will be amazed how much better you will feel.

Maybe you have 100 pounds to lose, or maybe just 10. Whatever the amount, remember to break it down to smaller goals. If you set a goal to lose 2 pounds a week, in a year you will have lost 100 pounds. Set safe, reasonable goals for yourself. A weight loss of one or two pounds a week is a healthy steady goal. Remember, we are deleting the repeat button in our lives. Make a commitment, no more yo-yo dieting!

It's Over for Here!

Week One Notes and Reflections...

_____

_____

_____

_____

_____

_____

_____

_____

Your favorite quote of the week:

_____

_____

_____

_____

Week Two

Spend time reflecting and organizing your surroundings. God will not bless your mess. Clean up your home, office, car, purse and anything else that needs it. While you are cleaning and discarding this is a great time to reflect and really see where you are. Open up all of your mail and organize it. Enjoy the process! This is one project where you can see the fruit of your labor immediately.

Prepare and freeze an entire meal. During one of your busier weeks this will be a special treat.

It's Over for Here!

Week Two Notes and Reflections...

_____

_____

_____

_____

_____

_____

_____

_____

Your favorite 'feel good' song of the week:

_____

_____

_____

_____

Week Three

Now that you can literally see your way through some of
the clutter in your life, analyze your life right now. What
are your strengths? What are your weaknesses? What
things are missing or broken? What challenges are you
facing? Are there any immediate storms? Go through the
10 Steps to Get out of a Rut. Identify a plan and start
working it.

It's Over for Here!

Week Three Notes and Reflections...

_____

_____

_____

_____

_____

_____

_____

_____

Your favorite Bible verse of the week:

_____

_____

_____

Week Four

Seek information. The internet and libraries have free information on any topic you could imagine. There are internet blogs, newsletters and talk shows that provide excellent advice on how to organize and maintain order in your surroundings. Find a method you can commit and stick to.

Utilize your calendar to make sure you log in projects and meet deadlines. This is also an excellent way to make sure you do not over commit yourself. Cramming too much into your schedule will cause some of your old habits to creep back in. By simply organizing your life, you can cut down on stress and frustration. You will begin to focus more clearly and feel good about your accomplishments. Learn to say no when you should.

Do not feel guilty for carving out some time for yourself. Time for yourself is mandatory! It could be as little as getting up one half hour earlier or taking the scenic route home or even hogging the bathroom with a good book!

It's Over for Here!

Week Four Notes and Reflections...

_____

_____

_____

_____

_____

_____

_____

Your favorite funny quote of the week:

_____

_____

_____

_____

Week Five

If there is any way possible, distance yourself from toxic people! If it is not possible to physically distance yourself, you can "guard your heart" and not allow callous and insensitive people to rock your world. People who try to rule others by intimidating, insulting and devaluing them have their own issues, often low self-esteem or other insecurities. As you develop and enhance a healthier self-image, you will find that their opinion of you is just that, their opinion.

Re-evaluate toxic relationships and make any necessary adjustments. As you become more of who God has ordained you to be, you will notice that people who cannot deal with the new you will eventually distance themselves.

If you are involved in any sinful relationship, severe it, as God will not bless your sin. Don't call Tyrone, leave him alone!

Reward yourself at different intervals. See how many ways you can stretch a $20.00 bill. Treat yourself to a Dollar Store Shopping Spree. You can frugally stock up that emergency closet. Everything does not have to have a monetary value. Eat your lunch in the park for a change. Spend a day at the beach or the library.

It's Over for Here!

Week Five Notes and Reflections...

_____

_____

_____

_____

_____

_____

_____

Your favorite Bible verse of the week:

_____

_____

_____

Week Six

Review the "Ten Things Grown Folk Ought to Have" list. Start somewhere. It may be as simple as stocking up on toilet paper for your emergency rations. Go to your favorite bargain store. With $20.00, you can start stocking your emergency pantry.

Be sure you start your personal emergency funds. Promise to never be broke again or suffer stress and distress because you did not have a simple $80.00 to replace or repair a car tire. Start with $20.00. Always keep $20.00 on you or available to you then increase it to $40.00, then $60.00, then $100.00. Start funding your cookie jar money and other savings as your individual needs dictate.

Make it FUN! Watching your emergency pantry fill up is encouraging. Make sure you check the Red Cross or other agency's suggested list of items to have on hand for an emergency as you stock your pantry.

It's Over for Here!

Week Six Notes and Reflections...

_____

_____

_____

_____

_____

_____

_____

Your favorite "victory" song of the week:

_____

_____

_____

Week Seven

Review week One through Six. Continue to journal your progress and your shortfalls. Don't be hard on yourself, keep revamping and revising your program. Utilize your creativity and enjoy the process. You are constantly moving away from areas of your life that are stagnant, destructive or barren.

As you continue to work your plans, attend free or low cost workshops in areas you need help with. Read books, study, learn and grow in your areas of interest. Volunteer where you can learn.

It's Over for Here!

Week Seven Notes and Reflections...

_____

_____

_____

_____

_____

_____

_____

_____

Your favorite quote of the week:

_____

_____

_____

Week Eight

Learn something new this week. It can be as simple as a new recipe or finally teach yourself how to fold fitted sheets or create balloon animals. Learning in itself is a challenge. Accomplishing something new brings on a good feeling.

Try a new exercise routine. You can often find exercise c.d.s in the clearance bins or even at the public library, or in your own collection of unused c.d.'s

Find a new park or section of the beach that you have never explored. Take a healthy sack lunch and a good book. Review your plan and tweak where necessary.

It's Over for Here!

Week Eight Notes and Reflections...

_____

_____

_____

_____

_____

_____

_____

_____

Your favorite Bible passage of the week:

_____

_____

_____

Week Nine

Spend quality time with a child or children. They always seem to liven up any atmosphere. If your children are grown, I am sure you can find some to borrow. If there are no children around… visit a senior family member or friend instead.

Continue working your plan! The journey to a new you can be exciting and exhilarating!

It's Over for Here!

Week Nine Notes and Reflections...

_____

_____

_____

_____

_____

_____

_____

Your favorite "empowering" quote of the week:

_____

_____

_____

Week Ten

Secretly, revamp your image. Seek out a style that more accurately reflects the evolving more confident more organized you. Have a private fashion show with the items you already own. See how many different ways you can wear your outfits. Create new ways to mix and match them. (Take pictures if you can do so inexpensively.) Now that your clothes are all out of the closet, use this time to clear out items that you no longer have use for and rearrange your closet so that you can have easy access to your "re-created wardrobe". Save the items that you may be able to sell at a yard sale or flea market. The proceeds from the sale you can use to pay down a credit card or boost your savings account. After the sale, unsold items can be donated to a tax deductible entity.

Psst...keep this project under wraps. (See Week Nine)

It's Over for Here!

Week Ten Notes and Reflections...

_____

_____

_____

_____

_____

_____

_____

_____

Thought of the week:

_____

_____

_____

_____

Week Eleven

Take a trip to a thrift shop or bargain bin and find one accessory that can enhance at least 3 outfits you already have. Your spending limit is $10.00. This takes discipline-but the "new you" can do it.

Continue to work on your image makeover from Week Eight. Keep a journal of comments or reactions you receive from family, friends or others. The clothes may be the same but you are strutting a new attitude! Have fun mixing and matching. Nine weeks is enough time to see some benefits from your hard work. You should be less stressed as you are learning techniques to de-stress your life. If you have changed you eating habits, perhaps you may even be in a different size. Strut your stuff!

It's Over for Here!

Week Eleven Notes and Reflections...

_____

_____

_____

_____

_____

_____

_____

_____

_____

_____

Scripture of the week:

_____

_____

_____

Twelve

Check your progress and reread this book. Make any necessary adjustments to your plan.

Review your journal. How is your life now? Write about it. What challenges do you face? Write down challenges you have overcome or at least areas you have made improvement in. Celebrate your progress, develop a strategy and set forth a plan to proceed further.

It's Over for Here!

Week Twelve Notes and Reflections...

_____

_____

_____

_____

_____

_____

_____

_____

Thought of the week:

_____

_____

_____

Be Encouraged.

You are preparing to

move forward!

"Here" represents any place or situation in your life that is stagnant, destructive or barren."

Chapter Twelve

Mops for Sale

12

Mops for Sale

One of my brothers once told me a story about a research project that was conducted in a mental institution. The researchers turned on a water faucet and let the water begin to flow over and flood the area in an adjacent room where the participants were sitting. Mops and buckets were in the room with them. As the water continued to flow into the room, those with a mental impairment kept mopping the water up. No matter how much water flowed into the room, they kept mopping. Mopping and probably complaining as the water continued to flow into the area.

Those who had a higher intellect, after some time, went into the other room to identify the source of the water and turned the water off.

How many situations in your life have you mopping and complaining year after year? Over the years, you may have changed mops, changed buckets and even changed your mopping techniques. Stop mopping and turn the water off! Remember, insanity is doing the same thing over and over and expecting different results. It's time for a change.

It's a Remix
A New and Improved You!

Do not be surprised if not everyone likes the new and improved version of you. Your shopaholic friends who used to hang out at the mall with you will not understand your new savings program. Your fast food frenzy friends will not understand your desire to brown bag it. Your couch potato friends might not want to get up off the sofa to take tennis lessons with you. Remember, gone are the days of pleasing others at your expense. Declare it's over for here. Everything stagnant, everything destructive and everything barren, it is over! Put up the mops, put up the buckets and move on.

With your new lifestyle remix, do not be afraid to dance to the beat of another drum. Stop prancing behind the Pied Piper and toot your own horn!

Surround yourself with growth and change. Remember, you have been in a place that was stagnant and barren for so long. Now that you moving away from "here" your surroundings should reflect it.

Some suggestions are:

- Buy a new plant for your office, (cubicles count).

- Find a new fragrance you like. Get free samples from the mall and wear it a day or two to see what you like, before purchasing it.

- Update your hair style to reflect your "new attitude"…only your hairdresser knows for sure.

It's Over for Here!

- Plant a herb garden on your kitchen window sill and use them for your new, health conscience recipes.

- Join the Y. They have more than just exercise classes.

- Create your personal dressing room complete with mirrors, seating, elevator music and all.

- Create a reading nook with comfortable seating and lighting.

- Drink your tea with the good china. Don't have any good china? Buy a cup and sauce from the flea market or yard sale.

- Use the good sheets.

- Create your own theme song! Rocky and Superfly aren't the only ones entitled to one.

- Buy new pajamas (bury the ragged t shirt).

- Keep your hands manicured. (Learn to DIY) Tootsies too.

- Make bath time luxurious! If you can not afford the whole set, you can buy one luxurious bath towel with matching wash cloth, spa/resort, pamper quality, perhaps even monogrammed.

- Treat yourself to fresh flowers often. They do not have to be expensive. During the summer, perhaps you can get them from your own yard.

It's Over for Here!

- Shop at the Farmer's market for fresh fruits and vegetables.

- Keep your home smelling fresh and inviting. Candles, oils, potpourri relax the mind and spirit.

- Anything broke and either can't be fixed or won't get fixed-trash it.

- Pick up a new hobby or side gig, or advance in an existing one. Keep in mind that all hobbies don't take a wad of cash to enjoy. You can learn to paint, sing, dance or sew. Do not go into debt to start a new hobby. It may be possible you can pick up some extra cash for your new hobby. I know a guy who earned pocket money in college by singing at weddings. Hmmm...

- Change the color or spruce up your bedroom. Wake up to beautiful surroundings.

- Keep your car clean and smelling fresh.

- Get a new calling card or update your business cards. You are too important to write your name, number and email on the back of a piece of junk mail in your purse. A crisp calling card, speaks volumes to new contacts. You can find great deals for cards online.

Keep in mind that it is your time to advance, enhance, be empowered, prosper and grow. Make the journey exciting!

Are You Ready?

Beloved, I pray for your successful exodus! The Promised Land lies just ahead. At this point, it does not matter how many years you have spent wandering in the wilderness. Whatever you do, do not sit and dwell on the miracles in the wilderness, those were for that time.

Do you remember the cemetery story? There is no exit to the left and no secret escape route to the right. Definitely, there is nothing behind in your past.

I close this book with great news! God has heard your prayers. The 9-1-1 call has gone up to Heaven. The huge iron gate is before you and you know what you have to do…move two feet. Once you step forward in faith, enormous gates of possibility will slide open. You have now buried those demons that have wrecked havoc on your finances, relationships and life choices all of these years. The skeletons in your closet are in their proper place, (six feet under). The fat lady just sang and the curtains have closed on all of the unnecessary drama in your life. Leap for joy as you exit those dead places in your life, for the final time. The marker reads, "Here lies the past, (**P**otential-**A**nemic, **S**tagnant **T**erritory). A glorious future lies ahead. Eureka! You have finally found it.

With the theme song of Rocky, playing in the background of your mind, you ought to be 'feeling strong now". Lace up your shoes, square your shoulders, loosen up your arms, even do the boxer's shuffle for a second or two. Now, with your head held high and your feet planted firmly on the ground, exuberantly exclaim to the world, Praise God, it's over for here. **THE END**

About the Author

Deborah A. Wright is a licensed evangelist, entrepreneur, avid writer, poet, storyteller, singer and actor who illuminates the stage with her witty and compelling, one-of-a-kind presentations. She travels frequently as a motivational workshop/retreat leader and is often requested to perform one of her one-woman theatrical presentations as "Lady Parablist", where she brings to life Biblical, historical and fictional characters. Deborah flows effortlessly from the woman at the well, to a suicidal crack addict to a rebellious clay pot at the mercy of the potter.

Deborah has produced and hosted local t.v and radio shows, with a Producer's Choice of the Year Award and a Minority Business Advocate of the Year award under her belt, to name a few. She has written her own inspirational business column for a community newspaper and served on the editorial board of another local newspaper as well as having served on over a dozen non-profit boards and was the recipient of an honorary doctorate in ministry in 2011.

Deborah is the creator and Host of a travelling Bible Study Gameshow called "Scrip-It". Not so celebrity contestants and zany characters, compete with teams in the audience for fun and prizes. Everyone has fun, and everyone learns just a little bit more about the Word of God. This gameshow is a wonderful evangelist tool.

Deborah has authored other books. Her other books include: *Don't Let the Gnat Knock You Out!, Pew Poetry* and, *So You Didn't Marry Boaz...How to Still Emerge as a Proverbs 31 Woman, Sometimes You've Got to Kill the Raven* and *The Year Uncle Bubba Jack Died...And Other Family Reunion Stories.*

Deborah A. Wright attended Michigan State University, with a concentration in Political Science and is also a Non Profit Specialist, specializing in helping organizations

It's Over for Here!

receive and maintain their tax exempt status by preparing 501(c)(3) documents, board training and compliance audits. Deborah is a native of Michigan and currently a resident of Ohio. Deborah is CFO of a nationwide Foundation that serves Churches and nonprofits in strategic planning and fiscal management and marketing.

Contact Deborah A. Wright for your next special event:

Parablist Publishing House, Inc.

www.parablistbooksonline.com

Email: parablistpublishing@yahoo.com

Email: datzwright@aol.com

Deborah A. Wright aka
Lady Parablist
Productions
Break Free!
www.ladyparablistproductions.com

Other Great Books by Deborah A. Wright

Available at:

www.parablistbooksonline.com

and

Amazon.com

MASTERING *the* ART *of* SUCCESS

LES BROWN MARK VICTOR HANSEN DEBORAH WRIGHT JACK CANFIELD

Deborah Co-authored with some the greatest motivators in the world Les Brown, along with Mark Victor Hansen and Jack Canfield, (Chicken Soup for the Soul duo)

"When the fairytale ends..."

So You Didn't Marry Boaz...

How to Still Emerge as a Proverbs 31 Wife

By Deborah A. Wright

So You Didn't Marry Boaz...
How to Still Emerge as a
Proverbs 31 Woman

(How to live out your God-assigned purpose even with a full plate and an empty cup.)

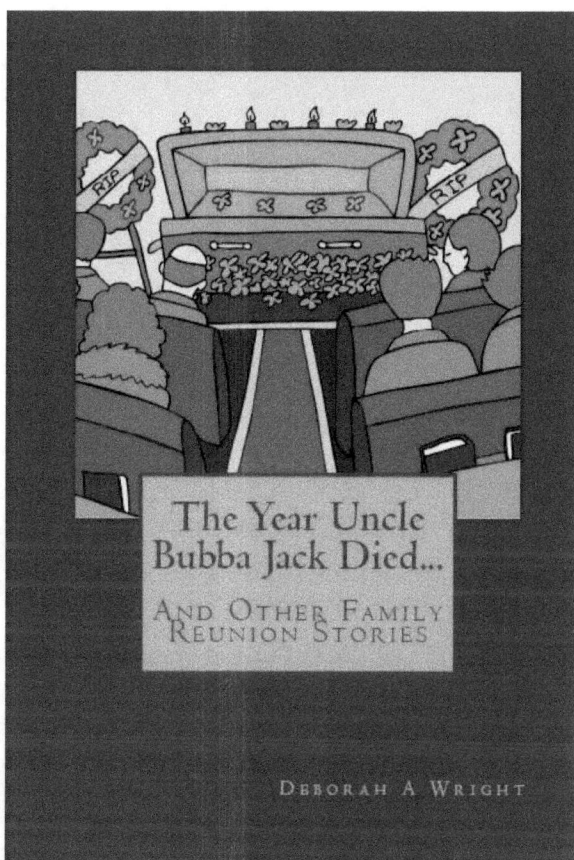

**The Year Uncle Bubba Jack Died
and Other Family Reunion Stories**

(A book of stories to be shared amongst family and
friends. It encourages storytelling; you can believe,
there is a storyteller among you.)

Sometimes You've Got to Kill the Raven!

Understanding
the Supernatural
Provisions of God

Dr. Deborah Wright

Sometimes You've Got to Kill the Raven!

(Understanding God's Supernatural provision in modern times.)

It's Over for Here!

Life was Great When I Was Eight
(A happy little children's story about birthdays)

Mr. Willie and the Raccoon
(A cute children's story about a quiet little neighborhood. But watch what happens once a raccoon decides to move in. Could this happen in your neighborhood?

It's Over for Here!

To invite

Deborah A. Wright

for your next

Workshop, Keynote, Revival,

Dramatic Performances,

Fundraisers

Or for other event ideas contact:

datzwright@aol.com

www.ladyparablistproductions.com

"Evangelizing the world…dramatically!"

134 | P a g e

It's Over for Here!

www.ingramcontent.com/pod-product-compliance
Lightning Source LLC
LaVergne TN
LVHW021511080426
835509LV00018B/2485